Reptiles

Belinda Weber

KINGFISHER

Contents

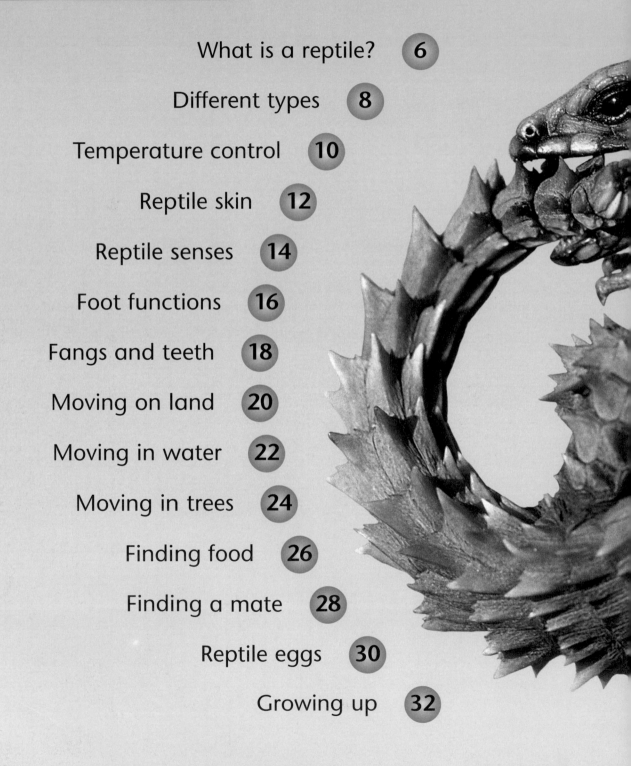

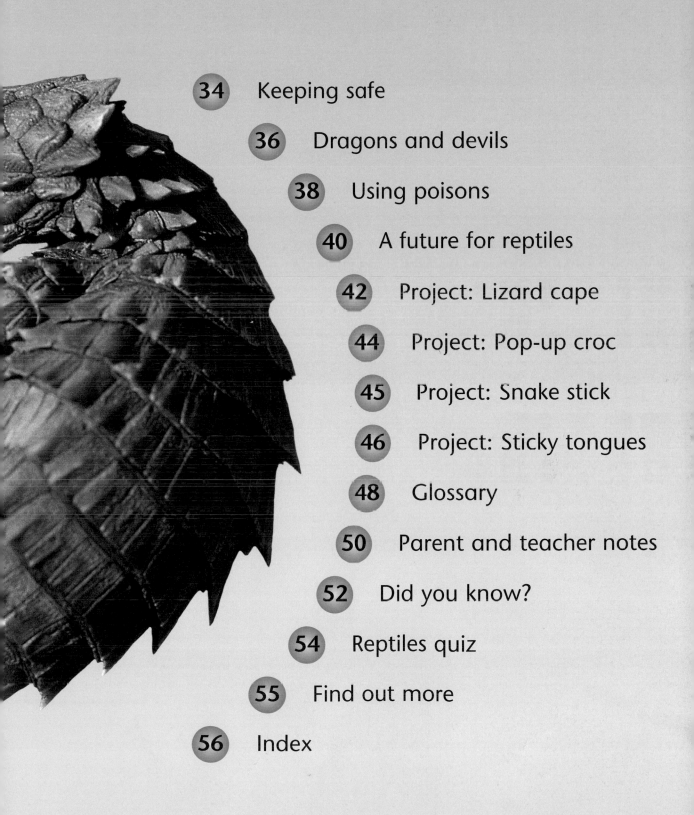

What is a reptile?

Reptiles are a group of animals with tough, scaly skin. They have a skeleton and backbone. There are more than 8,000 different kinds of reptiles.

Tough and scaly

Reptile skin is covered in thin, protective plates called scales, stronger than normal skin. Alligators have skin covered in thick, horny plates.

Water features
Crocodiles live near water. Like water birds, they have webbed feet to help them swim.

Different homes
All reptiles are suited to where they live. Alligators have a body for moving both in and out of water.

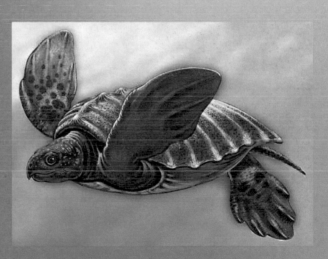

Prehistoric reptiles
Reptiles have prehistoric ancestors. Archelon was a giant sea reptile related to modern-day turtles.

Different types

Reptiles come in many shapes and sizes. Largest of all are the saltwater crocodiles, which grow to about seven metres long. Reptiles can be placed into four different groups.

Reptiles with shells

Turtles, terrapins and tortoises belong to this group. They all have hard, bony shells to protect the soft body inside.

Lizards and snakes

This is the largest reptile group.
There are more than 3,000
different species of lizards and
snakes found all over the world.

The crocodilians

Alligators, crocodiles,
caimans and gharials
belong to this group. They
can all move quickly over
land, but most are found
wallowing in water.

A group apart

Tuataras are the only members
of the smallest reptile group.
They are only found on
a few tiny islands
off the coast of
New Zealand.

Temperature control

Reptiles are cold-blooded, which means their bodies stay at the same temperature as their surroundings. They lie in the sun to warm up and hide in the shade to cool down. Once warm, they hunt for food.

Too cool to move

When some reptiles, such as rattlesnakes, find it too cold, they hibernate (go into a deep sleep) until warmer weather returns.

Keeping warm

Chameleons bask in the sun to heat up their blood. Reptiles need to be warm to hunt and digest their food.

Cooling off

A crocodile cools down by 'gaping' its mouth very wide. Or, it can take a dip in the river or lie in the shade.

Reptile skin

All animals need skin to stop them drying out in the sun. Skin also helps to protect the animal's insides from injury.

Spiky skin

Some reptiles, such as iguanas, have spikes down their backs to protect them from predators. These tough scales are made of keratin, the same material as our fingernails.

Smooth skin

Burrowing reptiles such as sandfish have smooth, flexible scales. These lie flat against the skin to help the animal slide into its burrow.

Growing bigger

A snake sheds its skin as it grows. It wriggles until it is free of the old skin. This is called sloughing.

Reptile senses

Senses help animals understand their world. All animals use their senses to find food, keep safe and find a mate. Most reptiles can see, hear and smell, and some can 'taste' things in the air.

eardrum

Listening lizards

Lizards do not have soft ears on the outside of the head like we do. They have an eardrum on each side of their head to pick up sounds.

Tasting smells

Many snakes and lizards flick out their tongues to 'taste' the air. A sense organ in the mouth works out what the tastes are.

Looking all around

A chameleon can move each eye on its own. This means the animal can look in two different directions at one time.

Foot functions

Reptiles exist all over the world, so they live in many different habitats. Their feet have evolved and adapted to suit their way of living. Some climb, some dig, while others can grip on to branches.

Spreading the weight

Giant tortoises have huge feet. As they clamber over sandy ground, their big feet help to spread out their weight so that they do not sink.

Gripping pads

This gecko is an excellent climber. Tiny, hook-like hairs on its feet (shown on the right) allow it to cling to almost anything.

Walking on water

Basilisks have wide feet and broad, scaly toes. They move at speed on these special feet to prevent them from sinking as they run across water.

Fangs and teeth

Some reptiles are small and hunt insects. Larger ones eat meatier creatures, such as mammals. All reptiles have a mouth and teeth suited to catching and eating their prey.

Snapping jaws

Alligator snapping turtles have sharp edges to their strong jaws. They snap them shut to slice prey into bite-size pieces.

Fold-away fangs

This rattlesnake has two sharp, hollow teeth called fangs, which unfold for biting. Poison is pumped through the fangs to kill the prey.

Catching fish

The mouth of the Ganges gharial is lined with small, sharp teeth. The teeth fit together tightly to stop fish from getting away.

Moving on land

All reptiles have a bony skeleton that helps to give their body its shape. Many have four legs, but snakes and some lizards do not have any legs. Most reptiles can move quickly to hunt or escape from danger.

Handling the heat

The Namib sand gecko has long legs. When it gets too hot, the gecko pushes up on these legs to lift its belly clear of the scorching desert sands.

Sidewinding

Sidewinder rattlesnakes wriggle and loop their body along the hot ground. This way, only a small part of the body touches the baking hot sand at any one time.

Inside a snake

A snake's skeleton has a flexible backbone with ribs attached. It is very bendy, so a snake can coil up or wrap around things.

Moving **in water**

Some reptiles live in water, while others swim to find food or to cool themselves down. All reptiles breathe air, so even those living in water have to surface from time to time to take in air.

Finding food

Marine iguanas are the world's only ocean lizards. They feed on seaweed and can stay underwater for about 20 minutes.

Graceful swimmers

Green sea turtles beat their front flippers like wings and use their back ones to steer. Their smooth shells help them to move in water.

Powerful swimmers

Saltwater crocodiles swish their long tails from side to side to push them through water. Their legs help them to steer.

Moving in trees

Many reptiles are good at climbing. Tree-living geckos have special foot pads for gripping slippery leaves, while some snakes have ridged scales for clinging to branches.

Clinging on

Tree snakes have long, strong bodies. They wrap themselves around branches and reach out into the open to look for predators or prey.

Gripping claws

Monitor lizards have strong legs and feet with long claws for gripping.

Leaping lizards

The flying gecko has webbed feet and folds of skin along its sides, legs and tail. It uses these to catch the air and glide.

Flying lizards

This flying dragon lizard has flaps of skin along its ribs, useful as 'wings' for gliding.

Finding food

Although some lizards eat only plants, most reptiles are carnivores, which means that they hunt other animals. Some reptiles, such as crocodiles, have a varied diet, while others eat just one type of food.

Elastic tongue
Chameleons grip on to branches. They have a long, sticky tongue, which they shoot out at high speed to catch any bugs they see.

Eating frogs' eggs

When the cat-eyed snake finds a cluster of frogs' eggs, it slurps up the whole sticky mass.

Leafy dinner

The Solomon Island skink is strictly a plant-eater. It climbs trees to feast on the fresh green leaves.

Fresh eggs

The African egg-eating snake swallows eggs whole. It pierces the shells in its throat, so as not to spill what is inside.

Finding a mate

When animals are ready to breed, they find a mate. Some reptiles use smell to attract a partner, while others use colours, sounds and even dancing. Many males fight to win a female.

Bright throat

This male anole lizard puffs up its colourful throat and nods its head up and down. This shows females he is ready to mate and warns off rival males.

Breeding dance

Speckled rattlesnake males prove their strength by wrestling. They are venomous (poisonous), but they do not bite each other.

Wrestling match

Using their tails for support, male monitor lizards rear up on their back legs and fight rival males. The weaker male gives up.

Reptile eggs

Most reptiles lay eggs with soft yet tough shells. The egg's yolk provides the developing young with food. The shell protects it from outside conditions.

turtle nest

This olive ridley sea turtle is laying about 100 eggs into a hole she has dug in the sand. She will return to the sea after burying them.

Breaking out

Developing snakes grow an 'egg tooth' on the tip of their upper jaw. They use this to pierce the egg's shell when they are ready to hatch.

Live babies

Some snakes and lizards give birth to live young. This lizard's Arctic home is too cold for eggs.

Growing up

Baby reptiles usually look like small versions of the adults. They are able to catch their own food as soon as they hatch. Some begin by eating smaller prey than the adults eat.

Digging for freedom
Newly hatched olive ridley sea turtles dig their way out of their sandy nests. They crawl as quickly as they can towards the sea.

Growth ridges

As a tortoise's shell grows, another ridge is added to the patterns. People can work out the animal's age by counting the ridges.

ridges

Caring mothers

Although a fierce predator, this female Nile crocodile is a caring mother. She gently scoops her babies into her mouth to keep them safe.

Keeping safe

Reptiles use many different tricks to stay hidden while out hunting or while resting. If startled, some pretend to be dead. Others show that they are poisonous by being brightly coloured.

Armour plating

An armadillo lizard has sharp, spiny growths on its skin. When threatened, the lizard grabs its tail and curls up into a spiky ball.

Hiding in leaves

Gaboon vipers have mottled patterns on their skin. This helps them stay hidden among leaf-litter.

gaboon viper

Too big to eat?

Frilled lizards have a flap of skin around their heads that they can raise up. This makes them look bigger and scarier if a predator attacks.

Dragons and devils

Lizards are the most successful group of reptiles and live in many different places. Some have developed into big and fierce predators. Others are much smaller and live in trees, or even underground.

Dragons with beards

When threatened, the bearded dragon puffs up a spiky flap of skin under its chin. This makes it look too big to eat.

Big dragons

Komodo dragons are the largest of all lizards. They can catch goats and pigs, but usually they eat carrion (dead animals).

Thorny devils

A thorny devil's spines and prickles protect the animal from attack. They also catch dew for the lizard to drink.

Using poisons

Many reptiles use venom (poison) to kill prey. Venom can affect the nervous system, the tissues of the body or even blood. Venomous reptiles may also use these poisons for self-defence.

Spitting cobras
A spitting cobra sprays venom out of its mouth. It aims for its enemy's eyes. The poison is very painful and can cause blindness.

A poisonous bite

Gila monsters are one
of two venomous lizard
species. Their venomous
saliva (spit) poisons prey
as they bite and chew.

Swimming snakes

Sea snakes are the most
venomous snakes in the
world. They can swim
underwater for up
to five hours.

Noisy rattles

Rattlesnakes twitch the
loose scales at the end
of their tail to make a
rattling sound. This
warns that their
bite is poisonous.

A future for reptiles

Many reptiles are in danger or face becoming extinct. We must learn how our actions may harm reptiles, and do more to look after them.

Harmful trade

Many reptiles are killed for their skins. The skins are then used to make wallets, boots and belts, or souvenirs for tourists.

Tracking reptiles

This loggerhead turtle is being fitted with a radio transmitter. Scientists will monitor its movements so that they can learn more about this creature.

Returning to the wild

This alligator was once caught and sold as a pet. Luckily, it was rescued and returned to its real home.

Lizard cape

Make your own frilled cape
The Australian frilled lizard defends itself using its neck frill (see page 35). Make one yourself to see how this special defensive system works.

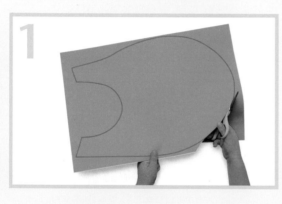

1

Draw one half of the frill shape on to a large sheet of coloured card. Use scissors to cut out the shape.

You will need
- Two large sheets of card
- Pencil
- Scissors
- Sticky tape
- Poster paints
- Paint brush
- Coloured tissue paper
- Glue
- String

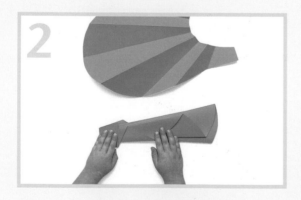

2

Make the other half of the frill with another sheet of card. Fold each half like a concertina.

3

Place the two halves together and join them using sticky tape at one end.

Create a pattern for your cape using paint. Cut out pieces of tissue paper and stick them on using glue to create a scaly texture.

Cut two long pieces of string. Attach them at either end of the cape – to the unpainted side – using sticky tape.

Place the finished cape around your neck and use the string to hold it in position. Give it a tug to raise the frilly cape and scare off your enemies!

Pop-up croc

Create a greetings card

Learn how to cut and fold paper to make your very own pop-up card. Then decorate it for a friend or relative.

You will need
- Coloured card
- Pencil
- Scissors
- Poster paints and brush

1

Fold the card in half and draw a zig-zag line for the croc's teeth. Cut along the line using scissors.

2

Fold the teeth shape out as shown, so that there is a definite crease. Unfold the card so that it lies flat.

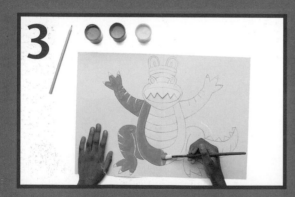

3

Draw out the rest of your croc in pencil and colour it with paints. Press out the teeth to make the card work.

Snake stick

Make a slinky snake toy

Snakes have a flexible backbone. Create this model, then use the stick to copy the way a snake coils and slinks over land.

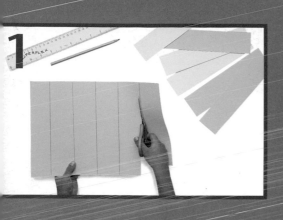

1

Use a ruler to draw out equal strips on the coloured card. Use scissors to cut out the strips.

You will need
- Coloured card
- Pencil
- Ruler
- Scissors
- Sticky tape
- Paints
- Paint brush
- String
- Wooden cane

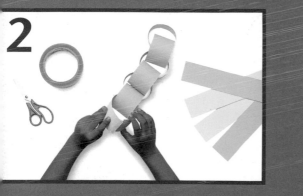

2

Using sticky tape, make one strip into a loop. Join other strips on in loops. Add a pointed loop for a tail.

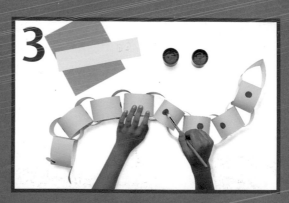

3

Add eyes and a forked tongue. Paint markings on. Stick one end of the string near the head and the other end to a cane.

Sticky tongues

Play at being a chameleon
Chameleons shoot out their sticky tongues to snatch up juicy bugs (see page 26). With this fun game, you can pretend to do the same!

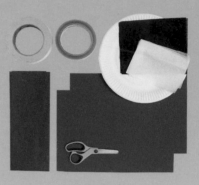

1

Roll up the sheets of card to make two tubes – one slightly thinner. Fasten the tubes using tape and paint them red.

You will need
- Coloured card
- Sticky tape
- Poster paints
- Paint brush
- Red tissue paper
- Black tissue paper
- White tissue paper
- Double-sided sticky tape
- Scissors

2

Slot the slightly thinner tube inside the larger one. Use sticky tape to hold the two tubes together.

3

Scrunch up lots of red tissue paper into a ball. Add strips of double-sided tape to make it sticky.

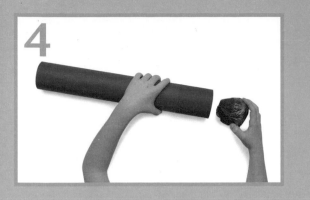

Push the ball of tissue into the end of the long tube. The double-sided tape should hold it in. This forms the tip of your sticky tongue.

Make flies by scrunching up smaller pieces of black tissue paper. Cut out wing shapes using white paper or tissue. Stick them on using tape.

Make two of these sticky tongues. Then, put all your flies into a bowl, or on a paper plate, and you are ready to play... The person who collects the most flies in one minute is the winning chameleon!

Glossary

Ancestor – an animal from which later animals have developed

Bask – to sit still in a warm area

Breed – to produce young

Burrow – to dig a hole to live in

Carnivore – meat-eating animal

Carrion – the dead bodies of animals

Coil – to wind round and round in loops

Developing – growing and changing

Dew – small drops of water that form in the night on grass and other plants

Digest – to break down food so that the body can use it

Eardrum – a part of the ear that sends sound vibrations to the inner ear

Evolved – changed over time

Extinct – when all animals of a certain type have died, and none are left

Flexible – bendy, stretchy

Flipper – limb that is suited for swimming

Glide – to float gently through the air

Habitat – the area where a plant or animal lives

Hatch – to break out of an egg

Keratin – a tough, horny substance found in hair, claws, fingernails and reptiles' skin

Mammal – a warm-blooded animal that feed its young on milk

Miniature – tiny

Mottled – patterned with different coloured patches

Nervous system – the network of nerves throughout an animal's body

Organ – a part of the body with a special job to do

Pierce – to prick and break into, or out of

Predator – an animal that hunts other animals

Prey – an animal hunted by another animal

Radio transmitter – a device that sends out signals that can be tracked

Ridge – a narrow, raised area on a flat surface

Saliva – clear liquid produced in the mouth

Skeleton – a framework of bones inside an animal's body

Species – a set of animals or plants with the same features

Startled – surprised

Venomous – full of venom, or poison

Wallowing lying still while floating in water

Webbed – webbed feet have toes that are joined together by a flap of skin

This book includes material that would be particularly useful in helping to teach children aged 7–11 elements of the English and Science curricula and some cross-curricular lessons involving Art.

Extension activities

Reading and writing
Read a legend or folk tale about a reptile. Some examples are the legend of St George and the Dragon, the Chinese legend of the Great White Snake and the Australian Aboriginal legend about how the Tortoise lost its tail and teeth. Draw two columns. In one, list ways that the reptile character is like a real animal. In the other, list ways that it is not. (Note: this information could also be displayed on a Venn diagram.)

Writing
Each double-page information spread has a title, introduction, and three paragraphs of text, each with its own sub-heading. Pages 8–9 show the four groups of reptiles. Create a table with facts and examples from each group.

Use pages 7, 16–17, 23, 24–25, 31 and 32 to prepare a report on the features and uses of reptile feet and flippers. What forces do they use? Find all the ways that reptiles move and create a table or report to describe them, with examples.

Creative writing: Read pages 30–31 and write a poem about being born from an egg. Imagine what your first view of the world might look like.

Speaking and listening
Read pages 12–13 about skin. What do humans do to protect their skin? Prepare a report on what you find.

Prepare a short speech on the reptile skin trade using information on pages 40–41 and your own research.

Science
This book links with the themes of habitats (pp6, 9, 11, 13, 16–17, 20–21, 22–23, 24–25, 26–27, 34–35), life cycles (pp13, 28–29, 30–31, 32–33), food chains (pp18–19, 26–27, 36–37, 38–39)

and forces (pp7, 13, 16–17, 21, 23, 24–25, 26, 29).

Page 7 says alligators can live in and out of water. What materials can you find that stay the same in and out of water? What materials change?

Compare the teeth described on pages 18–19 with human teeth. What is the same? What is different?

Cross-curricular links
Art and design
Page 15 explains that a chameleon can look in two different directions at the same time. Draw a picture showing what it would see.

Pages 34–35 have information about how reptiles use colours and patterns to hide or give a warning. Paint a picture that illustrates this.

Using the projects
Children can follow or adapt these projects at home. Here are some ideas for extending them:

Pages 42–43: Change your design to show a venomous or camouflaged reptile.

Page 44: pp8–9 show the four different groups of reptiles. Make more greetings cards by drawing an animal from each group on the front and gluing materials such as bits of torn paper, sandpaper or sequins to show its skin type.

Page 45: Add features such as ears, a tongue and fangs to your snake.

Pages 46–47: Could you change the design to make a tongue that can be blown out of the tube? Or can you make a reptile face and fix in a party blower so that it looks like the animal's tongue when you blow it?

Did you know?

- There are more than 8,000 species of reptile in the world, and they inhabit every continent except Antarctica.

- The king cobra can inject enough poison to kill an elephant.

- Komodo dragons can run at speeds of up to 20 kilometres per hour.

- A snake at a London Zoo was once fitted with a glass eye!

- Marine iguanas sneeze regularly to remove salt in glands near their nose. This salt often lands on their heads, giving them their distinctive white cap.

- Most of the world's snakes (nearly two-thirds) are non-venomous. Only 500 snake species are venomous.

- Geckos are born without eyelids. To stop their eyes from drying out, they lick their eyeballs with their long tongues.

The shell of a turtle is made up of 60 different bones all joined together.

Spitting cobras can expel their venom up to 3 metres.

Most snakes can dislocate their jaws to make it easier for them to swallow large prey.

Reptiles have been around for nearly 200 million years.

You can tell the age of a rattlesnake by counting the rattles on its tail.

- The oldest tortoise to have ever lived was called Tu'i Malila. Born in 1777, it died in 1965, aged 188 years!

- Veiled chameleons have a tongue that is 1.5 times the length of their body.

- The leatherback turtle is the largest turtle species. Adults can grow to an average length of two metres and weigh up to 700 kilograms.

- Crocodiles swallow stones to help grind up food in their stomachs.

Reptiles quiz

The answers to these questions can all be found by looking back through the book. See how many you get right. You can check your answers on page 56.

1) How many species of snake and lizard are there?
   A – 100
   B – 3,000
   C – 10,000

2) Which is the largest lizard in the world?
   A – The marine iguana
   B – The anole lizard
   C – The komodo dragon

3) Why do giant tortoises have big feet?
   A – To stop them from sinking in sandy ground
   B – To help them move faster
   C – To help them climb trees

4) What does an armadillo lizard do when it is threatened?
   A – It runs away
   B – It curls up into a ball
   C – It hides its head in the sand

5) How long can a marine iguana stay underwater?
   A – 30 seconds
   B – 5 minutes
   C – 20 minutes

6) What would scientists use to track loggerhead turtles?
   A – A mobile phone
   B – A radio transmitter
   C – An undercover detective

7) How many species of venomous lizards are there?
   A – 10
   B – 200
   C – 2

8) What is special about the basilisk lizard?
   A – It can run on water
   B – It can breathe fire
   C – It can fly

9) How do young snakes break out of their eggs?
   A – They use their claws
   B – They have an 'egg tooth' on their upper jaw
   C – They wait for the egg to crack

10) What do rattlesnakes do when it gets too cold in the winter?
   A – Migrate
   B – Grow thicker skin
   C – Hibernate

11) What is the most poisonous snake?
   A – The sea snake
   B – The king cobra
   C – The rattlesnake

12) What does the Solomon Island skink eat?
   A – Insects
   B – Birds
   C – Leaves

Books to read

All about Alligators by Jim Arnosky,
    Scholastic, 2008

Anaconda (Day in the Life: Rain Forest
    Animals) by Anita Ganeri, Heinemann
    Educational Books, 2010

Explorers: Reptiles by Claire Llewellyn,
    Kingfisher, 2011

Reptile (Eye Know) by Penelope Arlon,
    Dorling Kindersley, 2008

Reptiles (Usborne Beginners) by Catriona
    Clarke, Usborne Publishing Ltd, 2009

Snakes (Amazing Animals) by Jen Green,
    Franklin Watts, 2011

Places to visit

The Natural History Museum, London
www.nhm.ac.uk
The Natural History Museum has a
number of exhibits on reptiles, including
skeletons and models.

Bristol Zoo
www.bristolzoo.org.uk
The reptile house at Bristol Zoo has an
extensive range of reptiles on show as
well as numerous species of amphibian.

London Zoo
www.zsl.org
London Zoo has a large selection of
reptiles on show including komodo
dragons, a Burmese python and an
Egyptian tortoise.

West Midlands Safari Park
www.Wmsp.co.uk
The reptile house at the West Midlands
Safari Park has a diverse collection of
reptiles. The park also has regular
encounter days where visitors are able
to look at certain reptiles and snakes
outside of their enclosures under the
guidance of the park keepers.

Websites

BBC Animals
www.bbc.co.uk/nature/animals
This website has information about a
wide variety of reptiles from all around
the world. There are also video clips for
each animal from BBC programmes.

National Geographic
www.nationalgeographic.co.uk
On the National Geographic website you
can find out all about your favourite
reptiles. There is a wealth of facts on
snakes, crocodiles and lizards,
accompanied by some stunning
photographs.

British Reptiles
www.wildlifetrusts.org
The reptiles section of this website has
information about the species of reptile
that are found in the United Kingdom,
with details about their habitat and their
relationship with people.

Reptiles quiz answers

1) B	7) C
2) C	8) A
3) A	9) B
4) B	10) C
5) C	11) A
6) B	12) C